Original title:
Leaves of Longing

Copyright © 2025 Creative Arts Management OÜ
All rights reserved.

Author: Zachary Prescott
ISBN HARDBACK: 978-1-80566-733-9
ISBN PAPERBACK: 978-1-80566-862-6

Sighs Carried by the Gentle Current

A fish swam by with a curious grin,
It whispered jokes about the world within.
The river chuckled, bubbles in its flow,
As currents carried punchlines, all aglow.

A turtle tried to join the stand-up crew,
But his slow delivery just wouldn't do.
The frogs croaked loud, their laughter echoed high,
While dragonflies buzzed, like they could fly high.

The Unseen Garden of Thoughts

In a garden where thoughts play,
Butterflies giggle in a jumbled ballet.
Petals sneeze pollen, loud and quite strange,
While ants throw a party, all bound to exchange.

A worm tells jokes, with a wriggle and squirm,
As daisies join in, causing quite a squirm.
The sun chuckles softly, making shadows dance,
While hiccuping clouds spill their sweet, silly chance.

Murmurs of the Seasons Within

Winter whispers with a scoff and a cheer,
Wearing mittens made of nothing but fear.
Spring bursts in, tossing snowballs with glee,
While summer insists it's too hot for tea.

Autumn arrives with a rustle and sigh,
Tossing in leaves as if wanting to fly.
The seasons bicker over time's light shares,
While the clock tickles all with whimsical flares.

Flickers of Emotion on the Winds

A breeze tickles laughter through trees in a whirl,
While feelings take flight, like a kite set to twirl.
Joy dances in circles, while anger just frowns,
And confusion trips over its own silly gowns.

The wind wears a scarf made from giggles unbound,
Singing silly sonnets, oh-so profound.
Whispers of joy crash like waves on the shore,
As clouds share a wink, wanting the world to adore.

Timeless Echoes in the Rusting Boughs

Old boughs creak stories in whimsical tones,
With echoes of laughter mixed in with groans.
Rust hangs like memories, glittering bright,
As the moon tries to tickle both day and night.

Squirrels debate where the best acorns lie,
While owls roll their eyes, pretending to sigh.
Each crack of the wood tells a tale of the past,
As time winks mischievously; oh, how it lasts!

The Soliloquy of Silence

In the garden, whispers tease,
A frog croaks questions to the trees.
The daisies nod, with smug delight,
As squirrels plot their nutty flight.

A comedy of crickets reigns,
While beetles dance on window panes.
The quiet grins, a silly prank,
With laughter sprouting from the dank.

A statue blinks—a trick of light,
And shadows giggle, taking flight.
The daisies whisper, 'Did you see?'
While ants march on, so seriously.

Through silent echoes, fun prevails,
As nature spins its wobbly tales.
In laughter, whispers take their chance,
A soliloquy, a silly dance.

Moments in the Mist

In morning's fog, the world is shy,
A dog takes charge, its tail held high.
Puddles reflect a gloomy frown,
While ducks just waddle, never drown.

The mist rolls in, a ghostly prank,
As little gnomes escape the dank.
They giggle low as they peek through,
At walkers lost, in search of dew.

Umbrellas turn to flying ships,
And raindrops tease with silly flips.
The world seems lost, a funny scene,
Where every shadow can be seen.

Yet laughter breaks the morning gloom,
As friend and foe trip on a broom.
In moments misty, spirits lift,
A dance of joy, a morning gift.

Sketches of the Bittersweet

A toast to time, that's bittersweet,
With cake and crumbs beneath our feet.
The past parade of silly hats,
Ducks in bow ties and chubby cats.

From shadows sketching tales of yore,
To laughter rising, evermore.
The clouds drift by, like jokes untold,
As we sip tea that's getting cold.

With memories like flying pies,
And present moments, full of sighs.
A funny twist in life's own art,
Where bittersweet plays a merry part.

We paint our dreams in colors bright,
While laughter lingers, taking flight.
In sketches found in every heart,
The funny side's the best of art.

The Echoing Dance of Shadows

In twilight hours, the shadows play,
With pirouettes that steal the day.
A cat on tiptoes, oh so sly,
As dust bunnies leap and say goodbye.

Echoes of giggles float around,
As twilight lends a silly sound.
The trees bend low for a cheeky jig,
While fireflies join in wearing wigs.

The moon rolls in, a laughing sphere,
To join the fun, it winks and cheers.
And with each flicker, shadows sway,
In a dance that steals your breath away.

So join the echo, step in line,
Let shadows lead, it's quite divine.
In twilight's glow, laughter abounds,
With every step, joy knows no bounds.

Portraits of an Autumn Heart

In a park, I saw a crow,
Wearing shades, putting on a show.
'Don't mind me,' it seemed to say,
'Just living life my funny way.'

Squirrels danced with acorn dreams,
Plotting mischief in their schemes.
They giggled at the fallen leaves,
Creating jest from autumn eves.

Threads of Solitude

A lonely tree just stood and sighed,
In search of friends, it nearly cried.
'They've all gone away,' it thought,
'Except for me, and I'm quite fraught!'

A breeze whispered, 'Try a hat!'
The tree chuckled, 'Is that where it's at?'
With twigs adorned and branches wide,
It wore a smile with autumn pride.

The Cradle of Sweet Regrets

A balloon once flew too high,
And crashed, oh dear, into the pie!
'Not my fault!' the balloon exclaimed,
'It was the wind that played this game.'

Pumpkin spice went on a spree,
Chasing lattes with glee.
They spilled all over head and toes,
'This isn't what I chose!' it glows.

Gardens of Unspoken Truths

In secret beds where shadows lay,
The flowers giggle day by day.
They whisper truths, so soft and sweet,
'It's not our fault they can't compete!'

The daisies burst with laughter bright,
While roses swoon, a comical sight.
They poke fun at the busy bee,
'Thank goodness we're so fancy free!'

The Solitude of Rustling Petals

In the garden where soft whispers play,
A flower once danced till it lost its bouquet,
It laughed at the wind with a giggle, a twirl,
Yet forgot how to stand, oh, did it unfurl!

Among the daisies, a clumsy bee buzzed,
It tripped on a petal and turned a bit fuzzed,
The petals all chuckled, 'Oh dear, what a sight!'
And danced with the breeze till it dark turned to light.

The blooms throw confetti in shades of pure glee,
While a snail speeds by, laughing, "Catch up to me!"
But alas, poor slow snail just drags on its shell,
Pretending it's racing, it's doing quite well!

In shadows of sunset, the blossoms confide,
With giggles and chuckles, they sparkle with pride,
For nature's a jester, with laughter in bloom,
And petals of joy will forever assume.

Garnet Reflections in the Twilight

As night tiptoes in with a slip and a slide,
Crickets in chorus begin their sweet ride,
A squirrel on a branch starts a stand-up show,
Joking with stars that begin to aglow.

Oh, a moonbeam arrives dressed in shimmering glee,
Making shadows dance, what a quirky decree!
A puff of a cloud tries to hide from the jest,
While echoes of giggles put night to the test.

With garnet hues spilling, the twilight conspires,
To turn ordinary moments to sweet chuckled fires,
And breezes like laughter flick through every tree,
As if the whole world is ticklish and free.

In this shimmering twilight of jests and delight,
Every moment can spark, every shadow ignite,
For where laughter lingers, the colors all shine,
In the echoes of twilight, our hearts intertwine.

A Tapestry of Time's Erosion

The clock's hands are caught in a giggling spree,
Tick-tock it laughingly mocks you and me,
While cobwebs crochet tales of humor and strife,
Each thread tells a story, the fabric of life.

Old trees share secrets in rustles and snaps,
Of squirrels who scheme but can't manage their maps,
With each twist and turn, they tumble and trip,
As memories weave with a whimsical grip.

Erosion's just ticklish, with each grain of sand,
Watching the world with a playful command,
The past shakes its leaves, not a worry in sight,
As moments dissolve like fog into light.

Yet here we are dancing, in echoes of cheer,
With mischief and giggles for everyone near,
For time's but a jester, in a costume of years,
And laughter's the rhythm, the cure for all fears.

Chasing the Colors of Yesterday

In a meadow of dreams where the colors collide,
The past is a palette, all mixed up with pride,
Chasing bright memories that dart like a flash,
Bobbing on breezes, they twirl in a dash.

Yesterday's laughter plays hopscotch with noon,
Skipping through flowers, composing a tune,
Time trips on its laces, a comical sight,
As shadows and sunshine get tangled in light.

With hues like a rainbow, they scamper around,
Each giggle a color that dances unbound,
In the chase of the moments, we find our delight,
For the colors of yesterday brighten our night.

So grab on a whimsy, take flight with a grin,
For inside every sorrow, a joke can be pinned,
In chasing these memories, we learn to cheer,
That laughter and color are always quite near.

Visions from a Shaded Glade

In a glade where shadows prance,
I saw a squirrel do a dance.
It twirled and spun with silly glee,
Chasing thoughts of nuts for tea.

A chattering bird with a bright red hat,
Said, "Why wear clothes? A feather's where it's at!"
He fluffed his wing, made quite a scene,
In nature's court, he was the queen.

The Lament of the Wandering Breeze

The breeze sighed softly as it flew,
"Oh, why do I tickle cows and dew?"
With a whoosh and a swirl, it shook a tree,
And laughed as the branches waved back with glee.

Each ticklish leaf told tales anew,
Of how they once danced with morning's dew.
"Oh, what a life — it's not all bad!"
But then it tripped over a mop, how sad!

Cascades of Memory

In autumn colors, memories race,
Like popcorn kernels in a wild embrace.
Popping and cracking, all happiness —
A handful of laughs, who could guess?

They tumble down like a jolly stream,
Chasing sunshine, living the dream.
Wobbling teacups in grand retreats,
While giggling squirrels steal all the sweets.

Whims of the Wandering Wind

The wind decided to throw a jest,
Made a tea party for the crazy best.
Cups of clouds and snacks on the go,
With cookies of rain, oh the show!

It whispered nonsense to the tall grass,
In rhymes that would make the daisies laugh.
"Oh, shall we dance on this sunny bow?"
As butterflies joined, with a cheeky wow!

The Crumbling Canvas

In a garden where grass wears a frown,
The paint on the canvas is melting down.
Squirrels giggle on branches so high,
While the sun sneezes clouds from the sky.

A pickle jar sits on a stool with pride,
It swears it can dance if you stand outside.
With laughter in paint, the colors collide,
As daisies declare they'll not hide their side.

A ticklish breeze plays hide-and-seek,
Twirling the flowers, causing a squeak.
While daisies and dandelions spin and twirl,
Even the tulips giggle and whirl.

Birds try to sing, but they croak instead,
Hoping to share in the humor spread.
With every brushstroke, the world comes alive,
A comical canvas in which dreams thrive.

A Journey Through Gossamer Dreams

On a train made of yarn, we roll along,
With pillows for seats, where we all belong.
The conductor's a cat, with a hat on his head,
As the wheels spin tales of adventure instead.

A rabbit in glasses counts stars up above,
While the moon winks down, like it's fallen in love.
Pancakes fall softly, like sweet little seeds,
They blossom like laughter, and fulfill all our needs.

Through cotton candy clouds, the wind takes a leap,
Dancing with giggles, it twirls in a sweep.
The engine's a whisk whisking dreams into sight,
As we travel through colors bursting with light.

With marshmallow passengers holding on tight,
Each twist pops a bubble of pure delight.
Together we journey, oh what a scheme,
On this train of delight through the land of a dream.

Flickering Lights Beneath the Canopy

Beneath the tall trees where shadows do play,
The fireflies burst into their nightly ballet.
They waltz with the breeze, in a dance so sublime,
Whispering jokes, like a soft chime.

A raccoon dons shoes, with moves that confound,
He moonwalks through leaves that swirl all around.
The owls start to chuckle with eyes so wide,
At antics of critters who take joy in pride.

As whispers of night call the crickets to tune,
Singing of laughter beneath the full moon.
Each twinkle a giggle, each breeze a soft tease,
Wrapping the night in its warm, playful ease.

With lanterns above, glowing soft like confetti,
The leaves join the dance; oh, aren't we so petty?
As the night gently fades and the sun lifts the veil,
A tale of delight woven fresh in the trail.

Emotions Like Falling Leaves

In the park where the laughter decides to descend,
A teetering toddler befriends the weekend.
With giggles that flutter, like whispers of cheer,
They tumble together, not knowing their fear.

A squirrel steals a hat, thinking it's grand,
But it's really a frisbee that flew from his hand.
As shadows dance lightly, the sun begins to sway,
Painting the ground where our fancies will play.

Twirling about, with their arms open wide,
They catch all their feelings as they twirl and glide.
With each tiny moment, a breeze swirls away,
Like confetti of laughter from thoughts gone astray.

And when autumn shows up with a soft, tender laugh,
Turning seasons to memories, what a splendid gaff!
Emotions like giggles forever will stay,
In the hearts of the children who danced here today.

Fragments of Fauna and Fantasy

In a world where squirrels wear hats,
A turtle races on roller skates.
Lizards play chess, don't ask for stats,
While owls share gossip on garden gates.

A rabbit hops on a disco beat,
While foxes dance in a silly line.
The hedgehogs form a jazzy fleet,
And giggle as the sun starts to shine.

With whimsical dreams in the air,
Bubbles rise from a fountain of goo.
Unicorns prance, without a care,
As pandas sip tea, oh what a view!

In this realm, nonsense does reign,
Where every critter has charm and flair.
So join the fun, but don't complain,
For laughter echoes from everywhere!

The Scent of Distant Echoes

A whiff of dreams on a windy flirt,
Where cats wear capes and dive to the ground.
Lemonade clouds in a crisply colored shirt,
While high-fiving bees buzz around!

A giraffe paints graffiti on sidewalks anew,
And elephants juggle with ice cream cones.
Rabbits in sunglasses, oh what a view,
While turtles deliver the mail with fine tones.

The grass tickles toes in the bright sunny gleam,
As frogs recite poems on lily pads wide.
Chasing the shadows like a wild daydream,
And laughter spills out like a joyful tide.

So follow the scent, where echoes reside,
In a land where the silly roams ever so free.
For in these sweet whispers, joy cannot hide,
And each merry heart sings its own quirky spree!

Flickers of Fading Light

At dusk, when shadows begin to dance,
A firefly plays tag with a wandering breeze.
Mice in tuxedos take a goofy stance,
While chipmunks debate about cheese degrees.

A glowworm leads, in a wobbly parade,
With moons made of marshmallows hanging low.
As twilight sneaks in with a mischief laid,
And snickers of laughter begin to flow.

The stars wink lazily and catch the gaze,
Of owls who wear spectacles quaintly framed.
They hoot out riddles in whimsical ways,
As clowns in the corner get happily named.

So chase the flickers till dreams come alive,
Where night unfolds tales that spin and twirl.
For in this soft glow, it's fun to thrive,
As the world wraps you up in a sparkly swirl!

The Pulse of Verdant Regrets

In gardens where daffodils wear frowns,
A worm copies dancers in woodlands blue.
Pillows made of grass soften the grounds,
While crickets sing tunes that feel brand new.

A snail carries baggage, quite the tall tale,
And rabbits lament their lost carrot stash.
While frogs with regrets hop without fail,
In hopes that their fate might change in a flash.

Trees whisper gossip with leaves full of sass,
As shadows confess all the fun they have had.
A hedgehog once lost in a game of grass,
Now ponders the wisdom of being so rad.

With every heartbeat, regrets come to play,
In a realm where laughter slips through the cracks.
So let's dance on the mistakes of the day,
And embrace all the joy, leaving none in the backs!

Beneath the Golden Boughs

A squirrel stole my sandwich today,
I chased him down the winding way.
He giggled, danced, with nutty pride,
While I just sighed and tried to hide.

The breeze it tickles, the branches sway,
As I debated my sandwich's fate.
He burrowed it deep in a leafy nook,
I'll never trust a squirrel, I suppose.

The sun spills gold on the grassy square,
While critters play, without a care.
I pondered life behind my tree,
Am I the jester? Is it just me?

So here I sit in my leafy chair,
With squirrel snack thieves giving me a scare.
I'll stockpile snacks, for you can't tell,
When a sneaky little pest will ring my bell!

The Dance of the Desiring

The grasshoppers' jig makes me wish to hop,
But my legs are heavy, and my hopes, they flop.
They leap with glee, while I sit still,
With dreams of a pirouette down the hill.

A butterfly flutters with elegant grace,
While I stumble on, trying to keep pace.
She winked and twirled, I lost my shoe,
She laughed and landed on the morning dew.

The daisies join in, a floral brigade,
As I sipped lemonade in the leafy shade.
I cheer them on from my sunny retreat,
While plotting how to make my own beat.

But alas, the ants make a conga line,
And I'm just here with snacks and wine.
I'll cheer them all, stick with my crew,
The dance of life can be quite askew!

Reflections in a Dried Stream

The water's gone and the rocks lie bare,
Yet frogs still croak, like they don't care.
A turtle snoozes, with dreams of rain,
And I wonder, is it all just plain?

With pebbles scattered and dust so fine,
I'm searching for clues in this dried-up line.
The fish are laughing at my landlocked fate,
In this former stream, aren't I first-rate?

I scribbled a note on a cobbled stone,
"Wish you were here," but I'm all alone.
The dragonflies buzz, basking in air,
While I'm just trying to act debonair.

So I'll sit a while, not move an inch,
'Till rain arrives, or I find a pinch.
The world's upside down, in this dried-out scene,
And I'm just a spectator, or so it would seem!

Hues of Heartache

The maples blush in a fiery show,
While I ache for ice cream and perfect dough.
Each swirl of color shouts like a clown,
Yet my feelings are tangled and upside down.

I saw a crow steal a pastry today,
And frankly, it brightened my somber play.
With wings flapping wide, it took to the skies,
Like it's savoring triumph, oh, what a surprise!

The orange and crimson parade on by,
While I sit here, munching my pie.
The colors laugh as I tip my hat,
To squirrels and crows; oh, imagine that!

So here's to the hues, both bright and blue,
A canvas of chaos and laughter too.
In the end, I'll giggle at what I've found,
Life's a funny thing, spinning round and round!

Resonance in the Rustle

In the park where squirrels dance,
They munch on acorns, not by chance.
A gentle breeze makes branches sway,
    As if they joke about their day.

Underfoot, the twigs do crack,
While cats pretend they need a snack.
The shadows play their silly games,
As sunlight tickles, calling names.

A gust of laughter from the trees,
Whispers secrets, hugs the breeze.
Each flutter brings a chuckle near,
As nature's humor whispers clear.

The playful rustle, oh, what fun,
A symphony from everyone.
So join the chatter, take a peek,
At leafy laughter, mild and weak.

The Map of Unfulfilled Wanderings

A map laid out on a bench so wide,
With candies dropped and nowhere to hide.
It shows a path to snacks galore,
But squirrels claim it—oh, what a bore!

Onward I trek, my snack in hand,
Yet every detour reveals a stand,
Of prancing leaves that run away,
Just like my plans on a rainy day.

I chase them down, but they take flight,
They twirl and spin, such cheeky sights.
My compass spins from laughter loud,
While trees applaud from leafy shrouds.

In this wild maze of chirps and quacks,
I find my joy and map relax.
Forget the snacks; let's dance instead,
With spirits high—no room for dread!

Between the Bark and the Breeze

A tree once told me, with a grin,
"Forget your worries; just dive in!"
The bark was rough, the leaves so bright,
In laughter's shadows, all feels right.

The breeze it whispers sneaky tales,
Of squirrel pranks and hidden trails.
Each rustle holds a quirky tease,
As if the branches joke with ease.

Beneath the shade, a gnome would joke,
"Who needs a cloak when you can smoke?"
He laughed so hard, the grass stood tall,
As mossy friends joined in the call.

So here I stand, with giggles near,
In nature's arms, I shed my fear.
With trees and whispers, life's a tease,
Between the bark and joyful breeze.

Nostalgia's Thicket

In a thicket where the grasses sway,
Memories play on a sunny day.
The daisies wink, the dandelions grin,
While bees and butterflies swirl and spin.

Recalling times of silly games,
When laughter echoed, calling names.
Each moment so vivid, it tickles the mind,
As if the past and present intertwine.

The shadows of yesteryears come alive,
In every rustling leaf, they dive.
Uncle Joe's wiggle, Aunt Sue's dance,
In grainy films, they take a chance.

So let us frolic and dance around,
In nostalgia's arms, our joy is found.
For in the thicket, often we see,
Life's bittersweet comedy is key!

Petals in the Wind

A dandelion danced by, such a clown,
It tickled my nose, then flew upside down.
With pollen as confetti, it made quite a scene,
While bees played tag, it was all so serene.

Oh, how it spun in the bright sunny glow,
Like a ballerina, with nowhere to go.
It missed its cue, tripped on a twig,
And plopped on my sandwich—oh, what a gig!

The grass was in stitches, they laughed so loud,
As the petals declared, "We're wild and unbowed!"
But the breeze gave a huff, and they swirled back,
"To grace the garden—or to stay on this snack?"

So next time you see one, give it a cheer,
For the laughter it brings brings us all near.
In the great dance of life, it takes quite the spin,
With petals as punchlines, let the giggles begin!

The Color of Distant Dreams

A funny hue painted the sky just right,
With purple kangaroos dancing in flight.
They bounced on the clouds, all giggles and glee,
Dreams in their pockets, just waiting to see.

My friend, the old turtle, nodded with grace,
As he juggled bright choices from an invisible space.
"Choose the lilac!" he quipped, "It's all the rage,
The pink swirls are good, but better for a stage!"

The wind played a prank, wrapped a scarf 'round my neck,

Tickled my thoughts—oh, what the heck!
The beauty of nonsense, a whimsical theme,
Under rainbows we'll paint, in the color of dreams.

So let's chase those fancies, with joy as our guide,
With colors so vivid, let laughter abide.
For life's but a canvas, with splashes and schemes,
In the color of dreams, reality beams!

Embrace of the Ageing Trees

In a forest of whispers, trees tell a joke,
Their branches all creaking, like an old, wise bloke.
"Stop shaving my bark!" cried an oak with a grin,
"Get closer, you'll see I'm just wearing thin!"

A willow rebelled, with leaves like a mane,
"Freedom of foliage! I won't entertain pain!"
And the pines chimed in, with their needles so fine,
"Age is just a number, we're feeling divine!"

With roots deep in mirth, their trunks full of tales,
They giggled together, while shaking their scales.
"Oh, let's throw a party!" the maple tree cheered,
"We'll sway to the rhythm of laughter, no fear!"

So here's to the forest, where joy never fades,
An embrace of old wisdom, beneath leafy shades.
Don't fret about aging—just hug it real tight,
With trees full of mirth, you'll soar to new heights!

Melancholy in the Maple

A maple sat brooding, in colorful hues,
Counting the squirrels, and all of their blues.
"Why must they scamper? Why run and then hide?
Can't they just lounge, in their nutty pride?"

The crows cawed a song, full of cheek and delight,
"Come join our parade, we'll dance through the night!"
But the maple just sighed, "I'll beam from afar,
As long as I thrive, beneath this odd star!"

With every lost leaf, it chuckled and thought,
"Perhaps I'll be funny—maybe I won't rot!"
A gust of the breeze made it shimmy and sway,
"No more melancholy! Let's party today!"

So the maple embraced all the silliness spun,
With laughter erupting, it finally won.
For life's just a jest, with giggles bestowed,
Even maples can dance on the whimsical road!

Whispers of Autumn's Embrace

In the park, a squirrel's chase,
Spilling nuts all over the place.
With acorns flying, they collide,
"Where's my snack?" the sad thoughts hide.

A gusty breeze plays silly tricks,
Ruffling hats like gentle flicks.
The leaves giggle in golden hues,
While jumping dogs dance with their shoes.

Shadows Cast by Distant Dreams

A shadow hops, a pumpkin rolls,
While snickering squirrels steal our souls.
Dreams of chill in cozy socks,
Yet freezy winds give us cold knocks.

Cats in coats prance down the lane,
Wearing scarves, they'll surely gain.
With laughter locked in every bite,
Distant dreams bring giggles at night.

Echoes in a Forgotten Grove

Amidst the trees, a chatter grows,
Where owls gossip in hushed tones.
A raccoon waves, "Come sit a while!"
As mushrooms sprout, they boast and smile.

Ghostly branches sway and twirl,
As rock bands of critters rock and whirl.
A moth breaks out in nervous dance,
Hoping for just one last chance.

Wistful Breezes Through Fallen Canopies

Whimsical winds tickle our cheeks,
While hiding in spots for playful peaks.
Nature's jester in crisp twilight,
Makes leaves laugh and take to flight.

Around the bend, a bench does creak,
As a sleepy cat starts to peek.
Chasing shadows, they join the fun,
In a world where silliness has begun.

The Yearning Grove

In a grove where wishes dance,
Swaying branches twist and prance,
A squirrel dreams of acorn pie,
While birds just laugh and flutter by.

Beneath the shade, a turtle sighs,
With great ambitions in his eyes,
But every time he starts to zoom,
He ends up napping, feelin' gloom.

In the nooks, a fox will plot,
For snacks that he can sneak and trot,
But every time he tries to creep,
A tree root holds him, makes him weep.

So here they yearn for brighter days,
In funny, twisty, leafy ways,
Each creature shares a hopeful thought,
And laughs about what time forgot.

Echoes in the Canopy

Up in the treetops, whispers spread,
A parrot's joke, a finch's dread,
They echo 'round from leaf to leaf,
With giggles causing endless grief.

A wise old owl with glasses thick,
Can't see the joke; he's quite the trick!
The younger birds just roll their eyes,
At dad jokes soaring through the skies.

The wind sings tales of missed romance,
As critters sway and do a dance,
With every rustle, secrets glean,
Of all the crushes left unseen.

Oh, how they yearn for silly glee,
In every echo of the tree,
Where laughter floats on gentle breeze,
And dreams hang heavy with such ease.

Shadows on the Forest Floor

In the forest where shadows dwell,
A shy little mushroom hides so well,
He dreams of being a broad-brimmed hat,
But fears the touch of a curious cat.

A hedgehog rolls with dreams of speed,
But when he moves, he can't quite lead,
For each small step leads to a fall,
And laughter echoes through it all.

A rabbit hops with plans so grand,
To leap and bound across the land,
But every jump goes awry,
He lands in brambles and starts to cry.

There's yearning here, but oh so sweet,
In every tumble, every meet,
Where shadows play, those funny things,
And giggles bloom like spring's fine wings.

A Tapestry of Sighs

In a patch where vines entwine,
A butterfly dreams, feeling fine,
Of splendid flights and pollen kings,
But stumbles on those pesky strings.

A fuzzy caterpillar lags,
With visions of what beauty brags,
He spins his tale in threads and sighs,
While ants just scoff and roll their eyes.

Beneath a sun-soaked leafy veil,
A beetle plots a grand detail,
To strut his stuff on grassy stage,
But trips and flips into a rage.

Yet through the giggles, dreams arise,
In squiggly forms, beneath bright skies,
A tapestry of hope is spun,
With laughter dazed and hearts still fun.

Starlit Whispers in the Thicket

In a thicket where shadows play,
Squirrels gossip, come what may.
They chatter about the moon's big sigh,
While fireflies wink and giggle nearby.

Crickets strum their evening tunes,
Thumping beats beneath the moons.
Frogs jump in, with croaks so bold,
As if to say, 'Let's break the mold!'

The wise old owl, perched on high,
Hoots jokes that make the breezes fly.
His feathery friends roll their eyes,
"When will he learn? He's no surprise!"

Underneath this starlit dome,
Every creature feels at home.
In the thicket, laughter swells,
As nature weaves its quirky spells.

The Tenderness Beneath

In the garden where daisies dance,
A worm wrote poems, given a chance.
He scribbles with his little tail,
While bees buzz by, spreading the tale.

Petunias blush in chatty rows,
Complaining 'bout the pesky crows.
With every peck upon their head,
They wonder why they get outspread!

A dandelion dreams to be a star,
But feels quite short—can't reach too far.
His friends just laugh, say 'Stay right here,
You're blooming fine, hold back your fear!'

Down below where laughter hums,
A thousand secrets twist and thrums.
Tender roots entwine so sweet,
In friendship's dance, they feel complete.

Stories Each Leaf Holds

A leaf sighed stories from the breeze,
Of runaway ants and cheeky bees.
With tales of squirrels and their stash,
How acorns turned to forth-with cash!

Each flutter tells a jolly jest,
Of mice who think they can outquest.
While shadows creep, the sun is bright,
It's all a laugh until the night!

The blushing buds tell of a crush,
A shy flower met a dandelion rush.
"Oh, stop!" they giggle, "Hold that thought,
What's next? A crown? Or a fancy plot?"

In every rustle, secrets twine,
With giggles laced like summer wine.
So gather 'round and lend an ear,
These leafy stories bring us cheer!

Elysian Echoes of Retreat

In quiet nooks where whispers meet,
A rabbit dreams of fancy feet.
He prances 'round in dapper style,
While watching frogs hop with a smile.

Chirpy sparrows squawk and tease,
Their version of a fashion spree.
With mismatched feathers, all a-bloom,
They strut around, proclaiming doom!

Under the oak, the shadows play,
A turtle thinks it's time for day.
But snoozes on, his head out flat,
While bugs fly by, and think, "What's that?"

In Elysian spots, the laughter rolls,
As creatures share their quirky goals.
Retreat from worries, let them be,
In nature's fun, we all are free!

Imaginary Sprouts of Desire

In a garden of dreams, I plant a seed,
It dances and twirls, oh what a speed.
A carrot in glasses, a tomato in shoes,
They chatter and giggle, sharing their blues.

With wishes for rain, they softly sway,
Frolicking freely, come what may.
But when it's too sunny, they all wear hats,
Joking 'bout veggies becoming steeped in chats.

The lettuce tells tales of a blustery day,
Of croutons and dressings that got carried away.
And peas in a pod sing a merry tune,
As they plot for a picnic under the moon.

Where all the sprightly veggies take flight,
In a wild salsa party, a true delight.
They blend up their flavors, a humorous spree,
Oh, what a garden of whimsy they'll be!

The Garden of Forgotten Memories

Once in a patch where time forgot,
Grew cabbages plotting a high-flying plot.
They reminisce tales of days gone by,
Of birds that wore hats, oh me, oh my!

With sun-soaked secrets tucked in their veins,
They laugh about daisies that danced in the rains.
A worm with a monocle, wise and so spry,
Shares stories of apples that floated in July.

Yet in the same soil, a pickle frets,
He recounts romance with spicy croquettes.
As tomatoes blush over heartstrings long lost,
They toast to the chives, no matter the cost.

It's a garden of echoes, a whimsical scene,
Where memories flourish, fitting and keen.
With laughter that tickles the roots of the ground,
In this funny patch, joy is always found!

Solitary Paths in the Quiet

On a quiet lane where shadows play,
A gnome with a grin wafts worries away.
He skips with delight on his floppy old feet,
Collecting the giggles, how silly, how sweet!

In solitude, he strolls with great flair,
Talking to flowers that don't seem to care.
A daffodil chuckles, a tulip just yawns,
While the daisies engage in their daily brawns.

But who can complain on such a fine day?
For squirrels throw parties in mischievous ways!
Acorns are snacks, while the breeze brings the fun,
As the gnome starts to dance, a whimsical run.

Even alone, there's a riot of glee,
In the meandering paths where no one can see.
With laughter that echoes through the tall trees,
Follow the gnome, have a chuckle, if you please!

The Essence of an Unseen Yearning

In a pot on a sill, a dreambird sits tight,
Chirping of hopes that are out of sight.
She wants to fly high, but her wings are too small,
So she tells plant puns, catching laughs from them all.

The thyme rolls his eyes, the basil can't breathe,
As the dreambird weaves tales of the lives they could lead.
"Let's mingle with clouds, let's dance in the sun!"
But the pot stops her soaring, oh what a pun!

Yet in the thick air of their merry banter,
She flickers and flutters with whimsical slanter.
A sprout pipes up, with boldness sincere,
"Why dwell in this pot when the sky's drawing near?"

So together they plot an escape from the mug,
With laughter and longing, and a heartstring tug.
For in their small world, they find a bright spark,
Of unseen adventures, and laughter in the dark!

Yearning for the Harvest Moon

Oh, the moon's a giant cheese,
Why must it tease and make us squeeze?
In search of bites, we stand and grieve,
While squirrels giggle, 'We won't leave!'

Beneath its glow, the pumpkins prance,
Do they know they're in a dance?
With every twirl, a night-time joke,
The harvest whispers, 'You're all broke!'

The owls hoot tales of midnight cheer,
While crickets play their tunes so clear.
We toast with cider, some mischief too,
As moonbeams laugh at me and you!

So when the sky glows bright and bold,
We'll gather stories yet untold.
With every bite of pie we take,
Remember: laughter's all it makes!

When Shadows Dance with Memories

Shadows flicker, whisper soft,
They love to wink and play aloft.
With every sway, they tease the past,
Did you hear that? It won't last!

Forgotten socks hang on the line,
Barefoot walking, oh what a sign!
Nostalgia's prank, it trips us right,
As shadows giggle through the night.

The chair creaks low, a ghostly jest,
Reminding us we need our rest.
We laugh with shadows, oh what a sight,
They talk of dreams lost in the light!

So if you feel a playful nudge,
It's just the past, not meant to judge.
Let's dance with laughter, spin around,
In shadowed bliss, joy will abound!

Remnants of Sunshine in the Veil of Dusk

As daylight fades, the sun winks out,
Twirling leaves, they toss, they shout.
They've had enough of summer's heat,
Dusk arrives, they skip marathon feet!

The sky blushes in shades of glee,
Crickets chuckle, 'Join the spree!'
Each twilight giggle, a sweet embrace,
A rendezvous with the night's face.

Wishes hung from a starry thread,
Dreams doze off in a leafy bed.
We grab the twilight's cold old snack,
And in the moon's light, say "Come back!"

So here we sit with hues that swirl,
In the fashion show of dusk's twirl.
With remnants bright of daylight's cheer,
We laugh as night begins to veer!

The Heartbeat of a Waking Forest

In the forest, a sleepy yawn,
Branches stretch with the coming dawn.
Squirrels tickle the sleepy breeze,
While squirrels giggle in oak's8788777 trees.

The underbrush holds tales to share,
Crickets sing while badgers stare.
With every rustle, secrets unite,
Each tree has jokes, they giggle tight.

The rhythm of roots pumps fun around,
A heartbeat in this leafy ground.
With every step, a whisper plays,
As nature chuckles in playful ways.

So join the woods and take a listen,
In every leaf, a dream's glisten.
The forest waits with joy to unfold,
Each heartbeat sings, let laughter be bold!

The Fragmented Forest

In a forest where all things twist,
The trees are playful, they can't resist.
They wiggle and giggle, it's no surprise,
As the squirrels plot, with twinkling eyes.

Mushrooms dance in a leafy parade,
While the wise old owl is completely delayed.
He hoots with laughter, in a light-hearted jest,
As a rabbit hops by, in drag as a pest.

Acorns drop down like rain in the sun,
Rolling and tumbling, they're all out for fun.
The whole forest chuckles, a comical scene,
In this wacky abode where the critters convene.

The wind whispers secrets, a playful tease,
As branches shake hands with the cleverly breeze.
The forest remembers, not just in dreams,
It thrives on the laughter, or so it seems.

Musings of the Absent Heart

My heart is a bird, in feathers it floats,
Looking for love notes tied to small boats.
But boats start to sink, oh what a disaster,
As my heart flaps about, moving much faster.

I thought I could find, a love that would bloom,
Instead, I have socks that just linger and loom.
They laugh in the drawer, tickling my toes,
As my heart pulls a prank, not caring who knows.

Dangerous games of misplaced affection,
My heart throws confetti, but has no direction.
So here I am sitting, with giggles abound,
In the realm of what-ifs, my heart's playground.

But I'll keep on musing, it's part of the fun,
With or without love, I feel like I've won.
So raise a toast to the times we forgot,
In the silly adventures, we find what we've sought.

A Tapestry of Time's Longing

Time weaves a story with a giggle or two,
Where seconds wear hats and the minutes are blue.
The clocks tick in rhythm, a funny charade,
As the past sends a postcard; it's totally swayed.

Remember the days when we had to wait,
Days spent in funny lines, food on a plate.
The seconds were snails, but we laughed all the same,
In the tapestry's thread, we played with the game.

Years twist like pretzels, a flavor so bold,
Times dancing around like it's all made of gold.
The memories giggle, not caring for age,
For the laughter is timeless, an evergreen page.

So here's to our past, with jokes on repeat,
In the fabric of time, it's a comedic feat.
We spin in the dance of the stories we share,
With a tickle of joy in the wisps of the air.

Underneath the Swaying Branches

Beneath swaying branches, a picnic ensues,
With ants playing tag, exchanging their blues.
They chatter and giggle while munching on crumbs,
While the grasshoppers sing out their silly drums.

The wind swings by, tickling everyone's face,
As butterflies join in a merry chase.
"Catch me if you can!" they flutter and squeak,
While the bees buzz around, taking a peek.

A squirrel rolls by, wearing acorn-shaped shades,
Sipping on nectar, in the sun's warm cascades.
He spins and he twirls, what a humorous sight,
Underneath the branches, full of delight.

So come join the laughter, bring a joke or two,
With critters and quirks, there's fun to pursue.
Underneath these branches, where mischief awaits,
Life's a comical journey, with no tiresome fates.

The Rustle of Forgotten Wishes

In the wind, they flap and fly,
Dreams misplaced, oh me, oh my!
A sock, a shoe, and some old gum,
Whispers of hope, all quite dumb.

Through the trees, they jiggle and sway,
Chasing after the dog of decay.
Old aspirations dance in a twirl,
While squirrels plot their next great swirl.

Pinecones drop with a thudding yawn,
As wishes drift, and the sun keeps on.
Imagined jets, but here lies a plane,
Covered in dust, the thought feels vain.

But hey, a giggle as they wander wide,
Just like me, they chase and slide.
With every gust, let laughter bloom,
For dreams may wander, but joy finds room.

Beneath the Sapphire Skies

Clouds whisper secrets, a giggling game,
They dress themselves in a silly name.
Blue cotton candy, fluffy and bright,
They float like it's a wild delight.

Birds fashion hats with a feathered flair,
As they dive down, no worry, no care.
A butterfly slips on a tutu of cheer,
In a world where we dance without fear.

The sun throws confetti that tickles our nose,
While daisies cheer in their frilly clothes.
And beneath this dome of laughter and light,
We twirl in joy, oh what a sight!

With giggles galore and colors so grand,
Nature's playground, a wonderland.
Each heartbeat echoes a playful rhyme,
Under the sapphire skies, sweet as a chime.

Secrets of the Fading Flora

Once in a garden, a flower turned gray,
Said, "I'm just tired; let's laugh and play!"
With petals a-flutter, it made a joke,
About bees who danced, then swiftly broke.

The tulips whispered sweet nothings in bloom,
While dandelions threatened to fill the room.
A rogue seed bobbed with a mischievous grin,
"Why be a weed when you could be kin?"

Old vines tangled in tales of the past,
Telling tales that would make you laugh fast.
They chortled through seasons, as time went round,
Finding joy in the soil, love unbound.

So let us chuckle with flora so fine,
In gardens where memories twist and entwine.
For laughter's the sunshine that helps us to grow,
In the secrets of nature that we both know.

When Silence Speaks

In the quiet, a giggle, a soundless cheer,
Where whispers of mischief bounce off the near.
Balloons float high in the silence divine,
Hiding from cats who think it's just fine.

A sock hops by with a joyful leap,
As crickets laugh and tumble, not a peep.
The trees pretend to listen so well,
While ants throw a party, let's ring that bell!

Then comes a breeze that rustles a leaf,
"Who said silence can't be a thief?"
Laughter it carries, wrapped in a sigh,
As echoes of giggles drift through the sky.

So when silence speaks, don't take it for gloom,
It may just be waiting to burst forth with bloom.
Embrace the quiet and dance in its grace,
For joy hides in whispers, a silly embrace.

A Haven of Memories Amongst the Thicket

In a tangle of twigs, where squirrels get spry,
Old Mr. Owl naps, with a wink in his eye.
The rabbits all gossip, they're quite the keen crew,
While frogs in their tuxedos sing out, "Ribbit, boo!"

A rustle in bushes, it's just a small hare,
But I swear it's a dragon, I stop and I stare.
Imagining battles, heroics galore,
When really it's just lunch, not a quest anymore!

The breezes are ticklish, the berries are sweet,
The sun faux pas' tan lines with all of its heat.
As butterflies frolic, so carefree and bold,
I chuckle, for life here is just like pure gold.

A childhood, untouched, in this feathery vale,
Where whispers of laughter in shadows regale.
Each memory crafted, amidst greenery bloomed,
In the thicket of merriment, joy is entombed.

Shadows of Dreams Intertwined in Green

In a world where the daisies all dance in the breeze,
And chipmunks in tuxes throw all the best teas.
The dreams of the daisies are everything bright,
While mushrooms hold conferences by lanterns at night.

The grass whispers secrets, oh what fun is this!
I prance past the daisies, not one did I miss.
A turtle named Clyde wears his hat just so right,
Believing he's suave, but he's slow as a fright.

The wind makes me giggle, it tickles my nose,
While ants draft grand schemes, wearing miniature clothes.
A day spent in laughter? It's just what I crave,
With shadows of dreams that we gleefully save.

The hues of the sunset paint all of our plans,
As creatures debate with their tiny, neat hands.
In this lively green theater, we sing and we play,
For the shadows of dreams bring a joy every day.

The Silent Call of the Distant Horizon

The sun yawns a stretch as it wakes from its bed,
While critters on bicycles race off with such dread.
A breeze brings old tales, of fluffs and of puffs,
While ants haul their treasures, say, 'Hey, that's enough!'

Clouds form a party, they bounce high above,
While bees in their beanies buzz sweet songs of love.
The grass holds its breath, as if waiting for stars,
While hippos in tutus fumble in jars.

In the faraway land, where daydreams reside,
The sunbeams all whisper, a twinkle, a glide.
With socks on the wrong feet, we march right along,
In pursuit of that giggle, where joys seem so strong.

So heed the horizon, with its silent call,
A reminder that silliness waits for us all.
Here laughter's the language, in colors and sounds,
As we chase the horizon where wonder abounds.

Whispers of the Withering

Among the old branches where silence may dwell,
The whispers of petals weave stories to tell.
Withering whispers play hide-and-seek,
Telling tales of mischief, quite humorous and cheek!

An acorn quite plucky decides it will sing,
With wobbly notes—it's a silly, stout thing.
While twirling in circles, it's losing its way,
Dancing with shadows until it turns gray.

The winds pick their favorites, as if in a chose,
While giggles erupt from the roots of each rose.
A tangle of laughter where vines intertwine,
In this whispered old garden, hilarity shines.

So pick up your smiles and toss them around,
For in withering whispers, pure joy can be found.
No age can dull laughter, nor silence its song,
In this garden of jest, you'll forever belong.

A Symphony of Sorrowful Colors

In gardens where shadows get lost,
The flowers are arguing, counting the cost.
Petals debating in purple and green,
Who's the most vibrant? Oh, it's quite the scene!

The sun whispers jokes to a wilting rose,
As daisies unite to wiggle their toes.
A bee with bad jokes buzzes by in a flurry,
While tulips get tangled, oh what a worry!

With every gust, a leaf takes a chance,
It flutters and dances, just trying to prance.
The grass laughs along, no need for a frown,
As petals play tag, all while upside down!

So let's toast to colors that struggle and sway,
In this symphony where laughter leads the way!
Who knew that the garden could host such a play?
Just remember, don't get too close or you'll stray!

Beneath the Weight of Wandering Clouds

Under fluffy blankets of drifting delight,
Clouds take a nap at the edge of the night.
One grumpy gray puffs out a disgruntled sigh,
While cotton-candy clouds giggle as they fly!

A thunderstorm chimes in with a snarky remark,
"I can rumble louder—let's make it a lark!"
The sun just rolls eyes, shining bright with a grin,
Saying, "Boys, it's just weather, don't take it on chin!"

Raindrops descend with a plop and a splash,
They race to the puddles, oh what a bash!
Wet socks are a given, but laughter's the prize,
As rain boots go splashing, much to the cloud's surprise!

So here's to the sky, with its whimsical ways,
Where even the storms can put on a display.
Next time you look up, watch the playful parade,
Beneath all that moisture, nothing's dismayed!

The Stillness That Follows the Storm

After the tempest, the world holds its breath,
While daisies emerge from the fray of their death.
The squirrels are gossiping, drying their tails,
In puddles of laughter, while nature exhales!

A rainbow shoots by, like it's late for a show,
While raindrops still cling to the leaves down below.
One grumpy old rock yells, "Who opened the gate?"
As sunlight now dances, it's really quite fate!

The wind picks up jokes that the trees like to tell,
"Why did the lightning bring thunder to yell?"
The branches all giggle, a musical tune,
As puffs on the breeze sew a sweet afternoon!

So raise a glass—cheers to the calm after noise,
Where nature rejoices with all of its toys.
In quiet together, the world spins anew,
Just laughing at storms, like they always do!

Reflections in a Dew-Dripped World

Morning slips softly, wrapped in a glow,
Dewdrops are winking, putting on a show.
A grass blade stumbles; it's trying to shine,
While a leaf takes a selfie, oh how divine!

The spiders are crafting their silvery threads,
While daisies nod off, resting their heads.
A ladybug poses, a star from above,
Making faces at flowers—hooray for their love!

Colors are dancing in crystal-clear pools,
As puddles reflect all the light of the fools.
Each droplet is laughing, a funny little sound,
As the sun gives a wink, spreading cheer all around!

So cherish the morning, with all of its quirk,
As nature reminds us, it's all just a perk.
In dew-dripped delight, we all can partake,
And dance with the sunlight—make no mistake!

A Mosaic of Melancholy

Once in a park, I saw a squirrel,
Stealing my sandwich, doing a twirl.
He danced on the grass, a nut in his paws,
While I just stood there, frozen like a statue's cause.

The sun was a jester, with rays that would tease,
Chasing my worries like a soft summer breeze.
A pigeon then cooed, as if in a play,
"Who knew that the park could distract me this way?"

With benches adorned in a patchwork of stains,
I laughed at the sky, where it drizzled its rains.
Each droplet a giggle as it tickled the ground,
Oh, the foolishness found when sadness is drowned!

In this canvas of chuckles, I painted my frown,
With hues of absurdity, turning it upside down.
The world spun around me, a carnival found,
In a mosaic of laughs, my melancholy drowned.

Echoing Hues of Desire

A wish on a star that threw me a grin,
Told me to dance like no one could win.
With a wiggle, a jiggle, and a hop on one foot,
I serenaded the moon and my dreams went kaput.

Oh, the joy of the night held a glimmering spoon,
Serving wishes and whims beneath a whimsical moon.
But a raccoon appeared, raiding my dreams,
Stealing my hopes, or so it seems!

The stars chuckled softly, like sparkly confetti,
While I chased my desires, a bit too unsteady.
But their laughter was warm, a playful embrace,
As I twirled with the shadows, lost in the chase.

Each whisper I heard in the night's soft desire,
Made me dance like a fool, my hopes all on fire.
With a skip and a hop, I befriended a breeze,
And together we laughed, just aimlessly at ease.

Twilight's Serenade

At dusk, the sky painted a puzzling new hue,
I sang to the owls while they looked askew.
The grass hummed a tune, it tickled my feet,
While shadows crept softly, oh, what a treat!

Crickets were crooning their nightly affair,
As I joined in the chorus, why did they stare?
With a hop, skip, and jump, I gave it my best,
A melodic catastrophe—who wouldn't be impressed?

The stars appeared late, all twinkly and bright,
Joined in the drama of my clumsy flight.
They blinked at my antics with twinkles and glee,
While I sang to the moon, "Why won't you dance with me?"

The night chuckled softly, a gentle applause,
As I fumbled through verses, lost in my cause.
Oh, twilight, dear friend, you break every stress,
Through laughter and music, I find my success!

The Bloom of Unfulfilled Dreams

In my garden of wishes, blooms grew so tall,
Yet none bore the fruit of a grand waterfall.
Instead, I found daisies dressed funny in hats,
And roses that giggled with mischief like cats.

A sunflower danced like it had something to say,
While daisies chuckled, "Who needs dreams anyway?"
The vines whispered softly, a tangled delight,
As I pondered my plight in the softening light.

Oh, the tulips complained, their colors askew,
Saying, "Join in the fun, don't take it so blue!"
So I snickered along with my whimsical blooms,
Transforming my garden into heartwarming tunes.

Though dreams may wither and wander like weeds,
Each chuckle and smile becomes all that I need.
In a patch of odd laughter, my hopes come alive,
With flowers so silly, it's here I will thrive!

Hidden Corners of the Canopy

In shadows where the squirrels play,
The thickets hide their jokes all day.
With laughter echoing through the trees,
A chorus sung by buzzing bees.

The owls hoot witty puns at night,
While raccoons dance in sheer delight.
They gather 'round for tales so tall,
In hidden corners, hearts enthrall.

The sun peeks through with playful glee,
Tickling ferns as they sway so free.
Laughter rustles the vibrant green,
In nature's stage, a lively scene.

So find your joy beneath the boughs,
Where humor lurks, we'll take our vows.
To cherish life with all its quirks,
In leafy realms where laughter works.

The Veil of Green and Gold

A cloak of shades both bright and bold,
Wraps nature's secrets, tales of old.
Between the trunks, the antics spread,
As chipmunks share their dreams in bed.

The sunlight dapples through the spray,
Like glitter on a young child's play.
Whispers tickle the timid vines,
Giggles float on cuckoo's signs.

The fawn pretends to know the score,
While turtles slow dance by the shore.
A comedy of errors here,
As clumsy critters shed a tear.

In this rich tapestry we find,
A humor only nature's kind,
With vines that twist in happy cheer,
A green and gold brigade draws near.

Reverberations of a Lonely Heart

The branches sway with tales untold,
Of love that once was fresh and bold.
Now echoes ring with a goofy sigh,
  As crickets croon their lullaby.

A heart once full now takes a break,
In search of joy with every shake.
The wind insists it has a plan,
To find a dance partner, oh man!

The moon winks down, a sarcastic friend,
As shadows bend and twist and bend.
Each leaf a wink, each rustle sparks,
  A hopeful tune playing in parks.

So let the lonely heart embrace,
The quirks of life, the silly pace.
In nature's stage, it finds its part,
With humor stitched into each heart.

Branches of Forgotten Sorrows

In hollows where the whispers dwell,
Old branches hold their private hell.
Yet humor sprinkles through the gloom,
As laughter pokes from every room.

The acorns drop with playful thuds,
While shadows giggle with the buds.
A weeping willow cracks a grin,
At all the chaos deep within.

With every sigh, the branches dance,
In rhythms of a broken chance.
They twist and twirl, a jolly crew,
Defying woes with comedic view.

For in these boughs of sorrows cast,
The joy of laughter holds them fast.
With stories spun and quirks to share,
They find their peace in humor's air.

Songs of the Sun-dappled Path

A squirrel danced on a golden groove,
Chasing shadows of one silly move.
The sun giggled as it peeked through,
Tickling the grass with a glimmering hue.

A butterfly joined in the merry chase,
Dancing round flowers with elegant grace.
The path sang softly, all joy and delight,
As the world turned into a playful sight.

Laughter echoed 'neath the wise old tree,
As branches waved like hands of glee.
Each step a jig, each breath a cheer,
Nature's jesters were all gathered near.

With every swirl, a giggle would sprout,
Even the leaves seemed to laugh out loud.
On the sun-dappled path where joy doesn't cease,
Life's funny ballet dances in peace.

A Symphony of Falling Hues

Now the orange plays peek-a-boo with the red,
Laughing as they swirl, not a care in their head.
Yellow chimes in with giggles and spins,
As cobalt blues join, like mischievous twins.

A concert of colors, the trees start to sway,
As the wind takes a bow, in a impromptu ballet.
The ground, a stage with a crunch-softened sound,
And all of the critters gather around.

Even the clouds want a piece of the fun,
Making marshmallow shapes in the warm autumn sun.
They giggle and float while the stars take a nap,
While leaves pirouette in a whimsical flap.

As hues kiss the ground in a colorful heap,
A joyful cacophony makes nature leap.
With twirls and with whirls, it's a radiant show,
A symphony of colors that laugh as they go.

The Trellis of Time

A vine tried to climb but got tangled in rhymes,
Singing songs of the past, like old nursery crimes.
The garden rolled over in laughter serene,
While the weeds popped their heads in, just for the scene.

The sunlight crept in, a curious mouse,
Tickling the shadows that danced in the house.
"Why hurry," it asked, "let's giggle 'til night?"
As the flowers agreed and smiled in delight.

The moments were stitched with laughter and cheer,
As a snail bragged about his slow pace, with no fear.
Time's trellis was woven with joy and with play,
And every tick-tock joined in on the fray.

From the fluttering leaves to the buzzing of bees,
The whole garden giggled, a fine, funny tease.
In this trellis of time, so silly and sweet,
Each moment a joke, each heartbeat a treat.

Petals of a Longing Heart

A flower dreamed big with petals so bright,
Wishing for an ice cream truck to roll by tonight.
With sprinkles and laughter in soft summer's grace,
It giggled at bugs that joined in the race.

"Hey there, dear pollen! Don't get too shy,
Let's hop from the garden and reach for the sky!"
But the ladybugs chuckled, "We've got tea to sip,
Why chase the clouds? Let's just take a dip!"

Every petal had hopes, silly dreams that they share,
Wishing for adventures beyond garden care.
Yet the sunshine reminded them, "You're right where you stand,
Embrace all the laughter; just look at this land!"

So they chuckled together, as birds sang along,
Life's quirky little moments, the universe's song.
These petals of longing, a funny little art,
Smiling wide, they claimed joy, right from the heart.

www.ingramcontent.com/pod-product-compliance
Lightning Source LLC
Chambersburg PA
CBHW071848160426
43209CB00003B/467